Daniel Ricketson

The Factory-Bell

And Other Poems

Daniel Ricketson

The Factory-Bell
And Other Poems

ISBN/EAN: 9783744709880

Printed in Europe, USA, Canada, Australia, Japan

Cover: Foto ©Thomas Meinert / pixelio.de

More available books at **www.hansebooks.com**

BY

DANIEL RICKETSON,

AUTHOR OF "THE AUTUMN SHEAF," ETC.

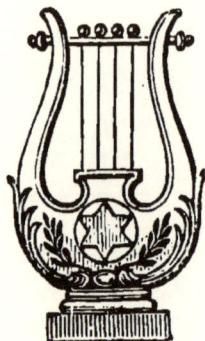

NEW BEDFORD:
E. ANTHONY & SONS, PRINTERS.
1873.

PREFACE.

THE object of these Poems is not to increase the distance between the employer and the employed; but to express a sympathy for a large and useful class of the community, through whose exhausting labors a great portion of the most important operations of our time are performed, in the hope thus to awaken a greater interest in their behalf on the part of those who have it in their power to relieve them from their heavy burdens, believing that in so doing the blessing of God would attend the much needed reform. Looking forward to the day, as I hope not far distant, when the hours of labor shall be essentially lessened, and the health, happiness, and the education of the operatives in the mills, and other laboring classes, receive greater consideration than at the present time, I contribute these humble efforts of my muse toward that end.

> "Ye friends to truth, ye statesmen who survey
> The rich man's joys increase, the poor's decay,
> 'T is yours to judge, how wide the limits stand
> Between a splendid and a happy land." GOLDSMITH.

D. R.

NEW BEDFORD, Sept. 1, 1873.

2

DEDICATION.

To the honest, industrious poor, and to all good and feeling hearts everywhere, these Poems are dedicated. If it be true that "what comes from the heart goes to the heart," I shall have no doubt of success in my undertaking."

May the shamrock, the thistle, the rose and the mayflower,
   At no distant day in sweet harmony twine,
And the nations of earth, thence forgetting their quarrels,
   Like brothers be guided by friendship divine.

POEMS.

INDEX.

THE FACTORY-BELL.

THE Factory-Bell is softly tolling,
　　Stealing through the Summer air,
Gently o'er the meadows rolling,
　　Reaching scenes of Nature fair.

But alas! its tones, though mellow,
　　Bring a sadness to my heart,
And the realms that these should hallow,
　　Take of shade and gloom a part.

For it calls from scenes of beauty,
　　From the lovely summer day,
Gentle hearts that often languish
　　For their native haunts away.

From green Erin's rural pleasures,
　　From stern Scotia's heather hills,
From old England's home-born treasures,
　　To the toiling of the Mills.

But for all, and blessed forever,
　　One o'errules the multitude,

The all-wise, the great Protector,
    Who from sin educes good.

Thus when fate seems unrelenting,
    And the way is dark and drear,   ₰
In the mist his arm preventing
    Keeps the lowly ones from fear;

Gives unto their hearts his spirit,
    Brighter than the noonday sun,
Wealth the poorest may inherit,
    Through his guardian mercy won.

But oh! ye who rule and dictate
    For your own base, selfish ends,
Nature and her God rebuke you,
    And at last require amends.

For the balances are nicely
    Fitted and adjusted true.
What man taketh God returneth;
    Naught escapes his sovereign view.

Still the Factory-Bell is ringing
    O'er the landscape, soft and clear.
I will trust that God is bringing
    With it hopes the sad to cheer.

THE IRISH-AMERICAN'S PLEA.

"ERIN GO BRAGH."

AH! were you exiled from your dear native
     land,
Your time and your life at another's command,
Ah! would you not think it uncivil indeed,
When for your just rights you would honestly
     plead,
Instead of kind words and brotherly love,
You should find those around you quick to reprove;
Or count it all wrong what your conscience deems
     right,
And look on your heart-cherished faith with
     affright?
No fault it can be, if we hither have come,
By the stern hand of fate, sad exiles from home,
To better our fortunes by honest, hard work,
In a land of the Christian, and not of the Turk.
And may we not surely add, too, our claim,
That "the earth is the Lord's," without any blame?
That "the fullness thereof" to his children belong;

Of whatever nation or kindred or tongue?
The Indian before you long held as his right,
The domain that you now possess in your might,
And he far away in the wilds of the West,
Seeks a home where the eagle buildeth his nest,
Away from the hand of intrusion and spoil,
While you are the lords of his ancestors' soil.
We are willing to work, but we also demand
The freedom once promised to all in this land.
Most surely the wrongs we so long have endured
In the land we have left, we hope will be cured.
Of your blessings we claim a very small part,
In return we assure a warm Irish heart ;
Our maidens are fair, and your sons soon will find,
By the great natural law, they're quite to their
          mind ;
So if in the future one race we shall be,
It surely is wise that we now should agree.
'T is love that gives justice, and no selfish end —
The spirit of Truth can in no wise offend.
Our God-given rights are the most that we claim,
And for this, most truly, we are not to blame.

THE IRISH FACTORY-GIRL.

SHE 's only a poor Factory-girl!
    That 's all, perhaps, you see,
Your lip in pride at her may curl,
    And scorn her low degree.

A poor exile from Erin's soil!
    That 's all of her you know;
Who in the Mill must daily toil,
    And trudge through rain and snow.

You see not through that dusty gown,
    Nor in that care-worn face,
The halo that o'er her is thrown,
    The mark of Nature's grace.

You see not there the noble heart,
    That beats to friendship strong,
The native charms, above all art,
    That to her soul belong.

But He who orders all things well,
    In mercy and in power,

Who bids the ocean billows swell,
  And paints the lowliest flower,

From out the humbler walks of earth
  Takes those the proud may scorn,
Nor heeds the heirs of wealth or birth,
  His favorites to adorn.

Such I have seen, such I have known,
  And such my soul admires,
Whose merit rare I gladly own,
  My simple song inspires.

Oh! may my sympathetic muse
  Such virtues still portray;
And from fair Nature ever choose
  Her aid to grace my lay.

THE IRISH-HEART.

THE Scotchman is canny, his virtues are many,
　　John Bull has in greatness his part;
But for warmth of affection, in the nation's election,
　　Stands foremost the kind Irish-heart.

From the north to the south, from the east to the
　　west,
　　Wherever his footsteps sojourn,
Just do him a favor, he 'll prize it forever,
　　And give you a score in return.

While others are ranging, and often are changing,
　　And thus stumble into the lurch,
His faith is unflinching, the years only clinching
　　The stronger his love of his church.

By nature so frisky, if he 'd leave but his whiskey,
　　And trust to his own hearty mirth,
Of all the good fellows on life's stormy billows,
　　He would rival the nations of earth.

B2

AN AMERICAN'S WELCOME.

OH! come from the banks of the clear-flowing
        Shannon,
    The Liffey, the Boyne, and the fair river Lee,
One heart shall at least extend you a welcome,
    And offer a home in the land of the free.

Oh! long, far too long! have ye met with derision,
    By those who would claim to be Christian and
            true;
'T is time we received you as brothers and sisters,
    And gave you as strangers the welcome your due.

For us ye have delved, ye have wrought, and have
            suffered
    The heat and the cold, for many a long year,
Oh! what now without ye, so strong and so hearty,
    Oh! what should we do, if ye no longer were
            here?

Let every kind heart come up to the rescue,
    And show unto others the rights they may claim,
My word for 't, you'll find a warm-hearted cheering:
    The praise of the poor is far better than fame.

THE EMERALD-ISLE.

HER fresh green fields rose to my view,
Her abbey walls, and turrets gray,
Her sparkling streams, and lakes so blue,
Fit scenes for loving hearts to stray.

Her fields of yellow waving corn,
The reapers busy at their toil,
The lark that hailed the early morn,
To cheer the tenants of the soil.

The milkmaid's simple, rural song,
The tender words of loving swain,
The healthful sports of old and young,
When harvested the ripened grain.

My friend, kind Andrew Donaldson,
With soft blue eye and honest face,
An exile from his native land,
To me these beauties would retrace.

I pitied him, so far away
From kindred, home, and all so dear,

And strove his rising sighs to stay,
  Or lend unto his heart some cheer.

Farewell ! old friend, long since the grass
  Has grown upon thy humble grave ;
My muse, withhold not as we pass,
  A tear for one so good and brave.

Farewell ! old isle of rich and poor,
  Mayst thou in no far distant days
Fresh blessings find for thee in store,
  And happier bard to chant thy praise.

A YOUNG IRISH WOMAN'S MEMORIES OF HOME.

WRITTEN AT HER SUGGESTION.

FROM the home of my childhood now far away,
    I fondly recur to the land of my birth,
The sweet native spot, the dear rustic cot,
    The scenes of my childhood, the dearest on earth.

Oh! well I remember, nor e'er shall forget,
    The beauty and freshness of all things around,
The meadow, the brook, and each cherished nook,
    The daisies and cowslips so often I found.

My labors were light, and my troubles but few,
    Though poor, we were honest and lived in
        content,
Our fare it was simple, our hearts they were true,
    And thankful for blessings a kind heaven sent.

But the day of misfortune at last on us fell:
    To cross the blue sea I left my dear home,

For the shores of old England, where we had heard
   tell
 Was plenty for all who hither might come.

No more the sweet air of my own native hills,
   No more the fair sight of fields waving with grain,
But the dust, and the smoke, and the noise of the
   mills,
   In exchange for the past awaken but pain.

Another long voyage across the broad sea,
   To the shores of the new-world an exile I come,
From the land of the oppressed to the land of the
   free,
   Where the poor and distressed may find a kind
   home.

And here, far away from Erin's dear isle,
   My mind oft revisits the scenes of the past,
And thus many hours else sad I beguile,
   But sorrow nor joy forever can last.

And so with my lot I'll strive for content,
   And new pleasures and friends be ready to find,
Still grateful for all by a kind heaven sent,
   For friendship and truth to no spot are confined.

MILL NOTES.—MOTHER AND DAUGHTER.

"SUSPIRIA DE PROFUNDIS."

Sighs from the deep.

Mother.

COME lay your head upon my breast,
   My darling, you are ill,
'T is Satur'-night, and take your rest;
   Forget awhile the mill.

You'll have the time till Monday morn
   To rest your weary head:
Oh! darling, sigh not so forlorn,
   Nor look as you were dead.

Daughter.

I know the rose has left my cheek,
   That once with freshness glowed;
Of things I now can rarely speak,
   Which once my spirit moved:

But while I'm lying in your arms,
   Dear mother, I am well;

Here I am safe from all alarms,
Nor hear the factory-bell.

Mother.

Sleep, then, loved one, I'll guard thy rest,
And bless thy spirit mild :
As calmly now upon my breast
Thou liest as when a child.

The mother, with a mother's love,
Long watched o'er her so calm,
Till nature from the realms above
Dropped down its heavenly balm.

Behold them there in that small room,
In one long, last embrace,
For gentle sleep hath sealed their doom,
And death hath left his trace !

O rich men, can you still enjoy
Wealth purchased at such cost,
Nor feel the canker of annoy,
Where so much good is lost?

The tale is one not overdrawn ;
Blame not the poet's lay,

Who would the oppressor thus forewarn
　　Against the judgment day.

And for the patient suffering poor,
　　The cause of mercy plead,
Bring faithfully before your door
　　The hearts you make to bleed.

In vain our churches we behold,
　　Their battlements and spires ;
A curse is on the glittering gold,
　　The fool so much admires.

Professor of the lowly Christ,
　　What profits, then, your prayer,
If unrebuked within our midst
　　Such sins pollute the air?

c

THE SCOTCH FACTORY-GIRL.

LASSIE, sweet lassie ! I mourn for thy lot ;
    The rose from thy cheek is fast fading away ;
How gladly I 'd send thee to thy dear native cot,
    Once more with thy mates 'mong the heather to
        play.

The daisies and blue-bells still bloom as before,
    The rivulet runs on its way to the sea,
The rose and the jessamine bloom by the door,
    And the mavis as erst sings his song from the
        tree.

Oh ! poor the exchange of the new-fashioned dress
    For the simple straw hat and coarse flannel
        gown,
Thy home in the fields with Nature to bless,
    For a life in the mill and the close crowded town.

O Scotia, beware how thou drivest away
    Hearts wedded in love to the dear native soil,

In far distant lands as a refuge to stray,
  And with down-fallen hearts among strangers
    to toil.

For these things I mourn, fair lassie, thy lot,
  And picture thee oft in thy childhood's dear home,
Again seated 'neath the old rustic cot,
  Nor wishing away from its comforts to roam.

But God still is good; let us keep this in view,
  And look unto Him, and to Nature so kind.
The fields here are green, the skies richly blue,
  Whose blessings, dear lassie, I hope thou wilt
    find.

One hand here at least in friendship I give,
  For every true heart from the land of dear
    Burns,
With a welcome and wish in plenty to live,
  And the blessings of God with the year's swift
    returns.

THE WAITING-MAID.

THOUGH but a simple waiting-maid,
   I see in her such neatness,
And in her gentle words and ways,
   There dwells so much of sweetness,

That I have said within my heart,
   " 'T is true, and nothing less,
That neatness is a virtue rare,
   And next to godliness."

I oft have seen those who are called
   By common rules more pretty ;
But rarely equal in the ways
   That grace this winsome " Ketty."

There's many a miss of higher rank,
   With wealth and pride o'erladen,
Who well might emulate the charms
   Of this sweet cottage maiden.

THE WEAVER'S SATURDAY-NIGHT.

TO M. P.

THE week's long hours at length are past!
   Its labors all are done.
With grateful hearts let us rejoice,
   The morrow is our own!

The bell shall not disturb our rest
   Upon that blessed morn;
The livelong day is all our own;
   Its pleasures who would scorn?

Our board is filled with wholesome food,
   The cloth is smooth and white,
The watchful dame, so kind and good,
   The stranger would not slight.

Permit me, then, with you to join
   In gratitude and praise,
To Him who ruleth everywhere,
   And thus our voices raise.

c2

We 'll sing the songs your fathers sung
   A hundred years ago,
For in this land of liberty
   Our hearts with joy may flow.

And while good cheer around is spread,
   Naught shall our comfort jar,
Nor will we e'er forget the dead,
   In " Erin " (dear) "go bragh ! "

We 'll take the harp from Tara's hall,
   Despite what Moore has sung,
And make it tell the tales of old,
   That once its strings outrung.

Thus welcome in the summer eve,
   Its starlight and its moon,
While join our hearts and voices strong,
   In some old favorite tune.

LINES

ON READING "THE SCOTTISH EMIGRANT'S FAREWELL."

THERE'S something wrong at home, O Scotland!
    When such brave hearts are torn from thee,
And bid farewell, once and forever,
    To seek a home beyond the sea.

Wouldst thou tear up thy mountain-daisy?
    Thy blooming heather, hare-bell blue?
Ah! then why crush or rend asunder
    Hearts to thy soil so leal and true.

Oh! ye whom Fortune's smile hath favored,
    Who hold the power to curse or bless,
Withdraw no more your kind protection,
    But save your children from distress.

The heart that loves thy hills and valleys,
    The music of thy feathered choir,
Deserves thy care and preservation,
    And should thy noblest zeal inspire.

Already they whose sires of old-time
  Stood by your sires in battlefield,
Are scattered through our western wide-world,
  And find protection 'neath our shield.

The Ægis of our state extendeth
  Its guardian power o'er all who seek
A safe asylum, and a welcome,
  Refusing neither strong nor weak.

Still unto thee, O valiant Scotland!
  The land of Wallace, Bruce, and Burns!
My muse would ask from harm to shelter
  The heart that to thy bosom turns.

No longer may thy sons be mourning
  For "bonnie-Doon," or "gurgling" Ayr,
But from thy ample stores returning,
  Find for their toil a liberal share.

But if thy peasantry destroyed,
  Like Erin's once her nation's pride,
As sang "sweet Auburn's" tuneful poet,
  They ne'er again can be supplied.

Oh! may such fate ne'er fall upon thee!
  Forefend thee Heaven from such dire harm!

And mayst thou take thy struggling children
   In love unto thy bosom warm.

Then shall thy soil rejoice in blessings,
   Then shall thy realm in peace abound,
Thy muse shall swell her song of praises,
   And music fill the air around.

"ENGLAND, FAREWELL."

SUGGESTED BY A PICTURE.

A MOTHER stood upon the deck, her boy,
  Her youngest, by her side, taking a last
Fond look of their dear native fatherland;
How sad the thoughts that crowd into her brain,
Thoughts of her childhood home and parents dear!
Brothers and sisters, every chosen spot,
Now rise before her mind, and sick at heart
She turns away, to hide the falling tears.
Oh! hard the fate that drives away from home
Hearts so attached, to seek in lands afar,
Amid the wilderness or forest rude,
By labor and by suffering, to gain
The livelihood denied on parent soil.
From off the shore the wind is blowing strong,
Filling the sails; and dashing on her course,
The brave ship hastens to her destined port
Across the broad Atlantic's watery waste.
No more the village green and ancient church,
Or ruined tower with clambering ivy clad,

Shall greet their eyes ; but in their stead behold
The wonders of the deep, with dangers dire,
Oft threatening to o'erwhelm their struggling bark.
Or landing safely on the distant shore,
Amid new scenes, new faces, all unused
To customs so peculiar, and so strange
To habits all confirmed in other lands,
Much there to suffer and much there to learn,
How fierce the struggle even here for food !
But not all dark ; the picture oft is bright,
And where the heart is brave and hands are strong,
A comfortable and a prosperous home
Is often made, and children reared to toil,
Become established, and become attached
To the new world, prefer it to the old.
Another instance of o'erruling power,
Converting seeming evil into good.
Mourn not, then, O dear exile ! for the home
Thy childhood knew ; but look with fresher hope
Upon the home adopted by thy choice.
Here may thy children and thy grandchildren,
To remotest times, find peace and plenty.

TO T. S.

AFTER READING HIS MANLY PROTEST AGAINST THE
EXISTING EVILS OF GREAT BRITAIN.

WHEN England drives from off her shores
     Such minds as these, through woe and want,
And keeps at home such countless bores,
     Who for their own ends ceaseless rant,—

There 's little hope that her success,
     In whatsoe'er is great and good,
The Lord of justice e'er will bless,
     Or guard her from vicissitude.

But ye are welcome, honest hearts !
     There 's room and plenty for you here,
And while the sun his warmth imparts,
     From tyranny ye 've naught to fear.

For every man to vote is free,
     The ballot-box is our stronghold,
Then from your prison barriers flee,
     And come within our ample fold.

WHITSUNTIDE.

OF old our ancestors on England's shores,
　　In the sweet rural districts and in towns,
Enjoyed, methinks, more cheerfulness of heart
In their religion, and yet found no loss,
But rather gain in the most vital part,
Linking the highest duties of the church
With harmless mirth and sweet poetic grace.
Christmas and Easter then were days of joy;
The huge yule-clog blazed in ancestral halls,
And merry dances led the joyful hours,
While healthful games at Easter cheered the year.
And so at each return of Whitsuntide,
While not forgetful of the sacred rites
Due to the church as on the other days,
Bedecked with flowers borne on the lap of May,
They bade a welcome to the vernal year,
And found a sweetness in its sacred rites.

EQUALITY OF BIRTH.

THE poorest man that walks on earth,
　　Is he not, too, my brother?
And have we not a common birth,
　　The earth, our common mother?

Away! then, with all caste and pride
　　Of family or nation,
And gladly take him at your side,
　　Joint heir of God's creation.

What boots it if the world we gain,
　　And lose all else beside?
The Briton, Saxon, or the Dane,
　　Cannot be saved by pride.

Of but one blood our God hath made
　　The nations of the earth;
How weak our pride, then, to parade,
　　Of wealth, or power, or birth!

Better to go where poor men go,
　　And lie where poor men lie,

Than waste our days in mimic show,
  And basely thus to die.

Then reach me forth thy honest hand,
  Thou man of common clay :
I claim thee for the chosen band
  Who hail the rising day !

The day when God's great jubilee
  Shall echo far and wide,
And all the nations shall be free
  From tyranny and pride.

BURNS' PLAID.

OFT owre the hills and far awa',
  When glint the wintra e'en star,
The poet-pleughman held afa',
    Wrapt in his plaid,
To meet some frien', or bonnie lass,
Or by the chimla-lug to pass
The livelong e'en aboot the glass,
    Graced by his plaid.

Oft by the braes o' "bonnie Doon,"
Or winding Nith beneath the moon,
His loe-inspired lays he 'd croon,
    Safe in his plaid.
Nae doubt his lovely Highland maid,
When angry gusts gart her afraid,
He warmly rowed within his plaid,
    His bonnie plaid !

A GREETING.

FOR all good fellows everywhere
  My heart beats true and strong:
I see you with your faces fair,
  Though mingled with the throng.

I meet you on the broad highway,
  Where oft I walk alone,
When evening shades shut out the day,
  And brighter scenes have flown.

I know ye by your easy walk,
  Your voices full of cheer,
And often halt with you to talk,
  Or lend a listening ear.

A blessing on each honest soul!
  A hearty shake of hand!
Nor shall the base the world control,
  While ye adorn the land.

D2

THE DAISY.

TO A. R.

EMBLEM of innocence and love,
  The Poet's favorite of the field,
Thou dost my admiration move,
  And food for pleasant musing yield.

A welcome to New England's soil,
  Though sterner than thy parent sod,
Yet genial to the laborer's toil —
  The land our fathers sought of God.

Thou canst not bear the wintry cold,
  But shrink'st before the cutting blast,
Still mid our flowers more hard and bold,
  However rich, thou 'rt not surpassed.

Ah! much from thee, thou simple flower,
  Comes up before my musing mind,
The lover's charm, the poet's dower,
  While all in thee a beauty find.

The land of Burns, romantic Ayr,
    Where thou, sweet daisy, lov'st to grow,
Bedecking o'er its banks so fair,
    Where its clear gurgling waters flow.

Theme of the poet's choicest lay,
    Thou charming, bright "wee-tipped" flower!
I welcome thee, this wintry day,
    And gladly feel thy genial power.

God's teachers to the chastened soul,
    The fresh wild-flowers of field or wood,
That exercise a rich control,
    And move us ever for our good.

ROBERT EMMET.

"Warm in his death-wounds sepulchred."
— O'Connor's child.— CAMPBELL.

THOU noble soul! patriot most true and brave!
    A nobler son thy native land ne'er bore;
There was no hand, alas! thy life to save,
    A victim thou to a tyrannic power.

Mourn, harp of Innisfail! thy darling mourn!
    While here, across the broad Atlantic wave,
A sympathetic muse would in her turn
    A tribute pay to one so nobly brave.

A martyr thou to liberty and truth!
    Here in this western world thy cherished name
Has often proved a watchword to our youth,
    And stirred their hearts to emulate thy fame.

Mourn, harp of Innisfail! thy early grave;
    The genius of thy country, Erin, weep!
O'er his sad urn, ye willows, ever wave,
    Ye patriots everywhere his memory keep!

But not in vain! the fire thou there didst light,
Still in thy nation's bosom fiercely glows;
The cruel power that o'er thee cast its blight,
Prophetic of its future downfall bows.

FREE TRADE, FREE SOIL, FREE MEN.

HO ! for free trade, ye sons of toil,
   A commerce from oppression free,
The land ye till, in truth free soil,
   Yourselves the sons of Liberty.

Throw out the banner to the wind !
   Write on its folds the words so brave :
" Freedom to Trade, to Soil, to Mind !"
   And thus our Nation's honor save.

No more should selfish millionaires
   Control our nation's weal or woe,
But every one by goods and wares,
   Have equal chance in wealth to grow.

The evils of the older world
   Already thunder at our door,
And soon their bolts, in fury hurled,
   May seal our fate forevermore —

Unless aroused with might and main
   To meet the common foe of all,

The tocsin ring from hill to plain,
  Through every village, farm and hall.

Not chartered right, but human right!
  The right of every honest man
To reap the fruit of labor's might —
  The right to think, to work, or plan.

A currency upheld by gold —
  A paper dollar good at par —
A hundred cents, as was of old —
  No discount base its worth to mar.

'T is agriculture, first and best;
  'T is commerce from her chains set free,
Mechanic arts by freedom blest,
  That shall maintain our liberty.

Let not our land become the seat
  Of prisons for the exiled poor,
But seeking souls a welcome meet,
  And room within the open door.

No land monopolies should here
  E'er exercise their base control;
Nor corporations, far and near,
  Wreak on the poor their want of soul:

But ever worthy of his hire
    Let every honest laborer be,
And all whom higher aims inspire,
    Have equal rights on land or sea.

The wrong that to the poor is done
    Will not alone upon them rest,
But surely as the constant sun,
    Oppressor suffer with oppressed.

For He who orders all above,
    Hath so ordained the life of man,
That other than the law of Love
    Must ever find His sovereign ban.

'T is equal justice through the land
    That can alone insure success,
All else will prove a rope of sand,
    And fall before almightiness.

Repeal the laws that man hath made !
    Which now too oft protect the knave,
And give once more to toil and trade
    The rights that nature kindly gave.

www.ingramcontent.com/pod-product-compliance
Lightning Source LLC
Chambersburg PA
CBHW031817090426
42739CB00008B/1310